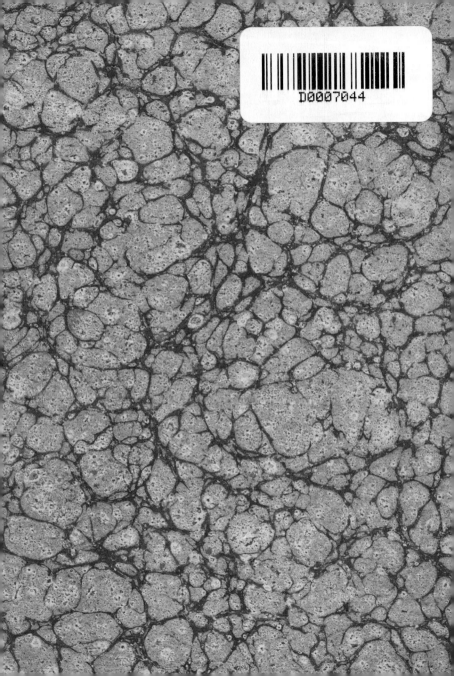

D0007044

THE WORDS OF
THOMAS JEFFERSON

THE WORDS OF
THOMAS JEFFERSON

MONTICELLO

The Words of Thomas Jefferson

This book was made possible by support from the
Martin S. and Luella Davis Publications Endowment.

© Copyright 2008 Thomas Jefferson Foundation, Inc. Second printing, 2011.

Th: Jefferson
MONTICELLO

www.monticello.org

All rights reserved. No part of this book may be reproduced in any form or by
any electronic or mechanical means, including information storage and retrieval
systems, except without permission in writing from the copyright holder, except
by a reviewer who may quote brief passages in a review.

Library of Congress Cataloging-in-Publication Data

Jefferson, Thomas, 1743-1826.
        The words of Thomas Jefferson.
            p. cm.
        ISBN 978-1-882886-27-2
        1. Jefferson, Thomas, 1743-1826--Quotations. 2. Jefferson, Thomas,
        1743-1826--Political and social views. 3. United States--Politics
        and government--1775-1783. 4. United States--Politics and
        government--1783-1865. 5. United States--Social conditions--
        To 1865. 6. United States--Intellectual life--1783-1865. I. Thomas
        Jefferson Foundation. II. Title.

E302.J442 2008

081--dc22   2008039681

THOMAS JEFFERSON
April 13, 1743 – July 4, 1826

CONTENTS

ABOUT *THE WORDS OF THOMAS JEFFERSON*

UNDERSTANDING THOMAS JEFFERSON and his significance begins with understanding his ideas. The varied programs of the Thomas Jefferson Visitor Center and Smith Education Center explore Monticello and address different aspects of Jefferson's impact on his world and on our own. Jefferson's words bring all of these experiences together.

The Robert H. and Clarice Smith Gallery, an integral part of the Center, contains four exhibitions. This book includes a selection of quotations by and about Jefferson chosen for the exhibition *The Words of Thomas Jefferson* featured in the Stacy Smith Liss Gallery. The exhibition is as much a work of art as it is a powerful means of conveying Jefferson's ideas. As visitors enter the space, key phrases are projected in light on the floor near words inlaid in the bluestone. These words are the subjects of quotations relating to Jefferson's ideas about the new nation. One by one, full quotations are projected on a wall.

The Words of Thomas Jefferson sets the stage for the use of Jefferson's words throughout the exhibitions. *Making Monticello: Jefferson's 'Essay in Architecture'* examines the architectural origins, transformation, and construction of Jefferson's house. Copies of drawings, pages from Jefferson's building notebooks, and excerpts of his correspondence demonstrate his innovative ideas about architecture. *Thomas Jefferson and 'the Boisterous Sea of Liberty'* traces the development and influence of Jefferson's ideas about liberty, emphasizing the Declaration of Independence and the global spread of freedom that Jefferson hoped would occur. *Monticello as Experiment: 'To Try All Things'* looks at Monticello as a complex community and especially as Jefferson's enlightened "laboratory" of ideas about progress. Here Jefferson put his scientific knowledge into practice, hoping that his experiments would advance the country he had helped to found.

As we look back on Jefferson from the vantage point of the twenty-first century, we are reminded that we inhabit a world shaped by his ideas.

SUSAN R. STEIN
Curator, *The Words of Thomas Jefferson*
Richard Gilder Senior Curator and
Vice President for Museum Programs
Thomas Jefferson Foundation

JEFFERSON'S USE OF LANGUAGE

THOMAS JEFFERSON WROTE LETTERS and papers on a bewildering variety of subjects, from agriculture, archeology, architecture, and astronomy to paleontology, philology, politics, and public education. The unifying element of this vast output was a graceful, spare, and lucid style that he took great pains to perfect and maintain. He evidently labored over drafts of most of his letters before recopying them in his letterpress and polygraph machines.

Jefferson sought to avoid repeating himself when he wrote comparable letters to different recipients. He celebrated living language and did not hesitate to welcome neologisms and coin words of his own, including belittle, monocrat, and neologize. Seeking to declare American independence in language as well as government, Jefferson adopted simplified spellings of some words, such as embarras and knolege, and eliminated linguistic exceptions by using "ie" even after the "c" in "recieved" and including an apostrophe in the possessive "it's." In what may have been a manifesto for republican simplicity, he also lowercased the beginnings of most of his sentences and such honorifics as "mr" and "mrs."

Jefferson was very consistent in his use of these writing conventions and he used them for a reason. In reproducing his words, we have chosen to reproduce them as literally and faithfully as possible. In order to insure that quotations follow the original manuscript exactly, all Jefferson quotations in these galleries have been checked character for character against the original manuscript by at least three trained documentary editors, using a combination of visual and oral proof readings.

Under the sponsorship of the Thomas Jefferson Foundation, the Retirement Series is preparing the definitive edition of Jefferson's letters and papers, including incoming correspondence, for the period between his retirement from the presidency in 1809 and his death at Monticello in 1826.

J. JEFFERSON LOONEY
Editor, *Papers of Thomas Jefferson: Retirement Series*
Thomas Jefferson Foundation

THE WORDS OF
THOMAS JEFFERSON

On America

America was conquered,
and her settlements made
and firmly established,
at the expence of individuals,
and not of the British public....
for themselves they fought,
for themselves they conquered,
and for themselves alone
they have right to hold.

A Summary View of the
Rights of British America
1774

my god! how little do
my countrymen know
what precious blessings
they are in possession of,
and which no other people
on earth enjoy.

To James Monroe
June 17, 1785

cultivators of the earth
    are the most valuable citizens.
they are the most vigorous,
      the most independant,
the most virtuous,
& they are tied to their country
    & wedded to it's liberty & interests
    by the most lasting bands.

To John Jay
August 23, 1785

…nothing in Europe can counterbalance
the freedom, the simplicity, the friendship
& the domestic felicity
we enjoy in America.

To Johann Ludwig de Unger
February 16, 1788

…we are not to expect to be translated
from despotism to liberty from
in a feather-bed.

To Lafayette
April 2, 1790

I can scarcely contemplate
a more incalculable evil
than the breaking of the union
into two or more parts.

To George Washington
May 23, 1792

I know no country where...
public esteem is so attached to worth,
regardless of wealth.

To Angelica Schuyler Church
November 27, 1793

we owe gratitude to France,
    justice to England, good will to all,
      and subservience to none.

To Arthur Campbell
September 1, 1797

it was by the sober sense of our citizens
that we were safely and steadily conducted
from monarchy to republicanism,
and it is by the same agency alone
we can be kept from falling back.

To Arthur Campbell
September 1, 1797

…I sincerely wish that
the whole Union may accomodate
their interests to each other…
that the wealth & strength
of any one part should be viewed
as the wealth & strength of the whole.

To Hugh Williamson
February 11, 1798

...the steady character of
our countrymen is a rock
to which we may safely moor...

To Elbridge Gerry
March 29, 1801

...to keep in all things within the pale
of our constitutional powers,
& cherish the federal union
as the only rock of safety;
these, fellow citizens, are the landmarks
by which we are to guide ourselves
in all our proceedings.

**To the Senate and House of
Representatives of the United States**
December 15, 1802

An equilibrium of agriculture,
manufactures & commerce
is certainly become essential
to our independance.

To James Jay
April 7, 1809

my affections were first
for my own country,
and then generally
for all mankind...

To Thomas Law
January 15, 1811

...before the establishment
of the American states,
nothing was known to History
but the Man of the old world,
crouded within limits either small or
overcharged, and steeped in the vices
which that situation generates.

To John Adams
October 28, 1813

no man has greater confidence,
than I have,
in the spirit of our people,
to a rational extent.
whatever they can, they will.

To James Monroe
October 16, 1814

On the subject of the history
of the American revolution,
you ask who shall write it?
…having been conducted by Congress
with closed doors,
and no member, as far as I know,
having even made notes of them.
these, which are
the life and soul of history
must for ever be unknown.

To John Adams
August 10, 1815

we are destined to be a barrier
    against the returns
        of ignorance and barbarism.

To John Adams
August 1, 1816

all entanglements with that quarter
of the globe should be avoided
if we mean that peace & jus[t]ice
shall be the polar ſtars
of the American societies.

To José Corrêa da Serra
October 24, 1820

Great Britain is the nation
    which can do us the most harm
of any one, or all on earth;
    and with her on our side
we need not fear the whole world.

To James Monroe
October 24, 1823

…the paper of July 4. 76.
was but the Declaration,
the genuine effusion
of the soul of our country
at that time.

To James Mease
September 16, 1825

THE WORDS OF
THOMAS JEFFERSON

—————⟶➤●⮜⟵—————

On the Arts

If there is a gratification
which I envy any people in this world
it is to your country [Italy] it's music.
this is the favorite passion
of my soul…

To Giovanni Fabbroni
June 8, 1778

Misery is often the parent of
the most affecting touches in poetry.

Notes on the State of Virginia
1782

you see I am an enthusiast
on the subject of the arts.
but it is an enthusiasm of which
I am not ashamed, as it's object is
to improve the taste of my countrymen…

To James Madison
September 20, 1785

from Lyons to Nismes
    I have been nourished
with the remains
    of Roman grandeur.

To Madame de Tessé
March 20, 1787

…Roman taſte, genius &
　　magnificence excite ideas…

To Madame de Tessé
March 20, 1787

music, drawing, books,
       invention & exercise
will be so many resources
       to you againſt ennui.

To Martha Jefferson [Randolph]
March 28, 1787

Architecture...is then
among the most important arts:
and it is desireable to introduce taste
into an art which shews so much.

Hints to Americans
Travelling in Europe
1788

I am but a son of nature,
loving what I see & feel,
without being able to give a reason,
nor caring much whether
there be one.

To Maria Cosway
April 24, 1788

they [women] have the good sense
　　to value domestic happiness
above all other, and the art
　　to cultivate it beyond all others.
there is no part of the earth where
　　so much of this is enjoyed
　　as in America.

To Anne Willing Bingham
May 11, 1788

do not neglect your music,
it will be a companion
which will sweeten many hours
of life to you.

To Martha Jefferson Randolph
April 4, 1790

...[Agriculture] this first &
    most precious of all the arts...

To Robert R. Livingston
April 30, 1800

no occupation is so delightful
     to me as the culture of the earth,
& no culture comparable
     to that of the garden.

To Charles Willson Peale
August 20, 1811

the new circumstances under which
we are placed call for new words,
new phrases and for the transfer
of old words to new objects.
an American dialect will therefore
be formed…

To John Waldo
August 16, 1813

THE WORDS OF
THOMAS JEFFERSON

On Conduct

An honest heart being the first blessing,
a knowing head is the second.

To Peter Carr
August 19, 1785

give up money,
give up fame, give up science,
give the earth itself & all it contains
rather than do an immoral act.

To Peter Carr
August 19, 1785

whenever you are to do a thing
tho' it can never be known
but to yourself,
ask yourself how you would act
were all the world looking at you,
& act accordingly.

To Peter Carr
August 19, 1785

honesty, knowlege & industry
are the qualities
which will lead you
to the highest emploiments
of your country,
& to it's highest esteem...

To Thomas Mann Randolph
November 25, 1785

the art of life is the art of avoiding pain:
      & he is the best pilot
   who steers clearest of the rocks & shoals
        with which it is beset.
      pleasure is always before us;
         but misfortune is at our side:
while running after that, this arrests us.

To Maria Cosway
October 12, 1786

the most effectual means
of being secure against pain
is to retire within ourselves,
& to suffice for our own happiness.

To Maria Cosway
October 12, 1786

…travelling is good for your health
and necessary for your amusement.

To Angelica Shuyler Church
July 12, 1788

…it is neither
     wealth nor splendor,
but tranquility & occupation
   which give happiness.

To Anna Jefferson Marks
September 21, 1788

we are firmly convinced
and we act on that conviction,
that, with nations, as with individuals,
our interests, soundly calculated,
will ever be found inseparable
from our moral duties.

Second Inaugural Address
March 4, 1805

The laws of humanity
make it a duty for nations,
as well as individuals,
to succour those
whom accident & diſtress
have thrown upon them.

To Albert Gallatin
January 24, 1807

…it has a great effect
on the opinion
of our people & the world
to have the moral right
on our side…

To James Madison
April 19, 1809

I find friendship to be like wine,
raw when new, ripened with age,
the true old man's milk,
& restorative cordial.

To Benjamin Rush
August 17, 1811

...nature hath implanted in our breasts
a love of others, a sense of duty to them,
a moral instinct in short,
which prompts us irresistibly
to feel and to succor their distresses...

To Thomas Law
June 13, 1814

…true wisdom does not lie
in mere practice without principle.

To John Adams
October 14, 1816

but time produces also corruption
of principles, and against this
it is the duty of good citizens
to be ever on the watch...

To Spencer Roane
March 9, 1821

THE WORDS OF
THOMAS JEFFERSON

On Education

experience hath shewn, that…
those entrusted with power
have, in time, and by slow operations,
perverted it into tyranny;
and it is believed that
the most effectual means
of preventing this would be,
to illuminate…the minds
of the people at large…

**A Bill for the More General
Diffusion of Knowledge**
December, 1778

...those persons, whom nature
hath endowed with genius and virtue,
should be rendered
by liberal education worthy...
to guard the sacred deposit
of the rights and liberties
of their fellow citizens...

**A Bill for the More General
Diffusion of Knowledge**
December, 1778

...wherever the people
        are well informed
they can be trusted
        with their own government...

To Richard Price
January 8, 1789

I cannot live without books...

To John Adams
June 10, 1815

enlighten the people generally,
and tyranny and oppressions
of body & mind will vanish
like evil spirits at the dawn of day.

To Samuel Du Pont de Nemours
April 24, 1816

…if the condition of man
is to be progressively ameliorated,
as we fondly hope and believe,
education is to be the chief instrument
in effecting it.

**To Eleuthère Irénée du
Pont de Nemours**
September 9, 1817

…untaught, and their ignorance
& vices will, in future life
coſt us much dearer
in their consequences,
than it would have done,
in their correction,
by a good education.

To Joseph C. Cabell
January 14, 1818

A system of general instruction,
which shall reach
every description of our citizens,
from the richest to the poorest,
as it was the earliest,
so will it be the latest,
of all the public concerns
in which I shall permit myself
to take an interest.

To Joseph C. Cabell
January 14, 1818

I know no safe depository
    of the ultimate powers of the society,
but the people themselves: and...
    to inform their discretion by education.
    this is the true corrective
    of abuses of constitutional power.

To William C. Jarvis
September 28, 1820

I look to the diffusion
of light and education as
the resource most to be relied on
for ameliorating the condition,
promoting the virtue and
advancing the happiness of man.

To Cornelius C. Blatchly
October 21, 1822

this institution of my native state
[University of Virginia],
the Hobby of my old age,
will be based on the
illimitable freedom of the human mind,
to explore and to expose
every subject susceptible of
it's contemplation.

To Destutt de Tracy
December 26, 1820

THE WORDS OF
THOMAS JEFFERSON

On Government

the whole art of government
consists in the art
of being honest.

**A Summary View of the
Rights of British America**
1774

Every species of government
has its specific principles....
It is a composition of the freest principles
of the English constitution,
with others derived from
natural right and natural reason.

Notes on the State of Virginia
1782

I have no fear that the result
of our experiment will be that
men may be trusted to govern themselves
without a master.

To David Hartley
July 2, 1787

...with all the defects of our constitutions,
whether general or particular,
the comparison of our governments
with those of Europe are like
a comparison of heaven & hell.
England, like the earth, may be allowed
to take the intermediate station.

To Joseph Jones
August 14, 1787

we can surely boast
    of having set the world
a beautiful example
    of a government reformed
by reason alone
    without bloodshed.

To Edward Rutledge
July 18, 1788

…whatever follies we may be
led into as to foreign nations,
we shall never give up our union,
the last anchor of our hope, &
that alone which is to prevent
this heavenly country from becoming
an arena of gladiators.

To Elbridge Gerry
May 13, 1797

...in time all these [states] as well as
their central government,
like the planets revolving round
their common Sun, acting & acted upon
according to their respective
weights & distances, will produce
that beautiful equilibrium on which
our constitution is founded...

To Peregrine Fitzhugh
February 23, 1798

politics & party hatreds destroy
the happiness of every being here.
they seem, like salamanders,
to consider fire as their element.

To Martha Jefferson Randolph
May 17, 1798

...error of opinion may be tolerated, where reason is left free to combat it.

First Inaugural Address
March 4, 1801

…every difference of opinion,
    is not a difference of principle.

First Inaugural Address
March 4, 1801

No provision in our constitution
ought to be dearer to man,
than that which protects
the rights of conscience
against the enterprizes
of the civil authority.

**To the Society of the
Methodist Episcopal Church**
February 4, 1809

no one more sincerely wishes
    the spread of information
          among mankind than I do,
and none has greater confidence
    in it's effect towards supporting
    free & good government.

To the Trustees of the Lottery
for East Tennessee College
May 6, 1810

the cement of this union
is in the heart blood of every American.
I do not believe there is on earth
a government established on
so immovable a basis.

To Lafayette
February 14, 1815

…man…feels that he is a participator
     in the government of affairs
not merely at an election,
    one day in the year, but every day…

To Joseph C. Cabell
February 2, 1816

...a government of reason
is better than one of force.

To Richard Rush
October 20, 1820

the equal rights of man,
and the happiness of every individual
are now acknoleged to be the
only legitimate objects of government.

To Adamantios Coray
October 31, 1823

…like religious differences,
a difference in politics
should never be permitted to enter
into social intercourse, or to disturb
its friendships, its charities or justice.

To Henry Lee [Draft]
August 10, 1824

THE WORDS OF
THOMAS JEFFERSON

On Knowledge

…ours are the only farmers
who can read Homer…

To St. John de Crèvecoeur
January 15, 1787

…read good books because
they will encourage as well as
direct your feelings.

To Peter Carr
August 10, 1787

Our laws, language, religion,
politics, & manners are
so deeply laid in English foundations,
that we shall never cease to consider
their history as a part of ours…

To William Duane
August 12, 1810

THE WORDS OF
THOMAS JEFFERSON

On Liberty

Under the law of nature,
all men are born free,
every one comes into the world
with a right to his own person,
which includes the liberty of moving
and using it at his own will.
This is what is called personal liberty…

Argument in
Howell v. Netherland
April, 1770

the god who gave us life,
    gave us liberty at the same time...

**A Summary View of the
Rights of British America**
July, 1774

...our attachment
    to no nation on earth
should supplant
    our attachment to liberty.

*Declaration of the Causes and
Necessity for Taking Up Arms*
June 26 – July 6, 1775

We hold these truths to be self-evident;
    that all men are created
        equal & independant,
that from that equal creation they derive
    rights inherent & inalienable,
        among which are
    the preservation of life, & liberty,
      & the pursuit of happiness...

Notes of Proceedings
in the Continental Congress
1776

I hold it that a little rebellion
now and then is a good thing,
& as necessary in the political world
as storms in the physical.

To James Madison
January 30, 1787

the tree of liberty must be
refreshed from time to time
with the blood of patriots & tyrants.
it is it's natural manure.

To William Stephens Smith
November 13, 1787

…the ground of liberty is
      to be gained by inches,
that we must be contented
      to secure what we can get
  from time to time,
and eternally press forward
    for what is yet to get.

To Charles Clay
Jaury 27, 1790

I would rather be exposed to
the inconveniencies attending
too much liberty than those
attending too small a degree of it.

To Archibald Stuart
December 23, 1791

this ball of liberty,
I believe most piously,
is now so well in motion
that it will roll round the globe.
at least the enlightened part of it,
for light & liberty go together.

To Tench Coxe
June 1, 1795

the last hope of
human liberty in this world
reſts on us.
we ought, for so dear a stake,
to sacrifice every attachment
& every enmity.

To William Duane
March 28, 1811

...the eyes of the virtuous,
all over the earth,
are turned with anxiety on us,
as the only depositories
of the sacred fire of liberty,
and that our falling into anarchy
would decide forever
the destinies of mankind,
and seal the political heresy
that man is incapable
of self government...

To John Hollins
May 5, 1811

if a nation expects
to be ignorant & free,
in a state of civilisation,
it expects what never was
& never will be.

To Charles Yancey
January 6, 1816

where the press is free
and every man able to read,
all is safe.

To Charles Yancey
January 6, 1816

the boisterous sea of liberty
is never without a wave.

To Richard Rush
October 20, 1820

in short, the flames kindled
on the 4th of July 1776.
have spread over too much
of the globe to be extinguished
by the feeble engines of despotism.

To John Adams
September 12, 1821

but the only security of all is
     in a free press....it is necessary
  to keep the waters pure.

To Lafayette
November 4, 1823

this was the object of the
       Declaration of Independance.
not to find out new principles,
      or new arguments,
    never before thought of,
       not merely to say things
which had never been said before;
    but to place before mankind
the common sense of the subject;
    i[n] terms so plain and firm...

To Henry Lee
May 8, 1825

the general spread
of the light of science
has already laid open to every view
the palpable truth
that the mass of mankind
has not been born,
with saddles on their backs,
nor a favored few booted and spurred,
ready to ride them legitimately,
by the grace of god.

To Roger C. Weightman
June 24, 1826

THE WORDS OF
THOMAS JEFFERSON

On Monticello

...I am savage enough to prefer
the woods, the wilds, &
the independance of Monticello,
to all the brilliant pleasures
of this gay capital [Paris]...

To Baron Geismar
September 6, 1785

and our own dear Monticello,
where has Nature spread
so rich a mantle under the eye?
mountains, forests, rocks, rivers.
with what majesty do we
there ride above the storms!
how sublime to look down into
the workhouse of nature, to see
her clouds, hail, snow, rain, thunder,
all fabricated at our feet!

To Maria Cosway
October 12, 1786

I am as happy no where else
    & in no other society,
       & all my wishes end,
     where I hope my days will end,
     at Monticello.
too many scenes of happiness
      mingle themselves
        with all the recollections
of my native woods & feilds,
    to suffer them to be supplanted
      in my affection by any other.

To George Gilmer
August 12, 1787

on the whole I find nothing
any where else in point of climate
    which Virginia need envy
to any part of the world....
    Spring and autumn, which make
    a paradise of our country...

To Martha Jefferson Randolph
May 31, 1791

I never before knew
the full value of trees.
my house is entirely embosomed
in high plane trees,
with good grass below,
& under them I breakfast, dine,
write, read & receive my company.
what would I not give
that the trees planted nearest
round the house at Monticello
were full grown.

To Martha Jefferson Randolph
July 7, 1793

I am then to be liberated
    from the hated occupations
      of politics, & to sink
into the bosom of my family,
      my farm & my books.
I have my house to build,
my feilds to farm, and to watch
    for the happiness of those
      who labor for mine.

To Angelica Shuyler Church
November 27, 1793

my books, my family, my friends,
       & my farm, furnish more than enough
to occupy me the remainder of my life,
       & of that tranquil occupation
most analogous to
my physical & moral constitution.

To Pierre Auguste Adet
October 14, 1795

it is now among
　　　my most fervent longings
to be on my farm, which,
　　　　with a garden & fruitery,
will constitute my principal
　　　occupation on retirement.

To Robert Livingston
January 3, 1808

...I shall retire into the bosom
of my native state,
endeared to me by every tie which
can attach the human heart.

To the General Assembly of Virginia
February 16, 1809

THE WORDS OF
THOMAS JEFFERSON

On Progress

...all the world would gain
by setting commerce at perfect liberty.

To John Adams
July 31, 1785

...letters are not the firſt,
but the laſt step in the progression
from barbarism to civilisation.

To James Pemberton
June 21, 1808

the contest...which ushered in
the dawn of our National existence
and led us through various
and trying Scenes, was for every thing
dear to free born man.

To the Republicans of Georgetown
March 8, 1809

there is a fulness of time
when men should go,
& not occupy too long
the ground to which others
have a right to advance.

To Benjamin Rush
August 17, 1811

I am not of the school
which teaches us to look back
for wisdom to our forefathers.
from the wonderful advances
in science and the arts
which I have lived to see,
I am sure we are wiser than our fathers
& that our sons will be wiser
than we are.

To John Wayles Eppes
February 6, 1818

when I contemplate
the immense advances in science,
and discoveries in the arts
which have been made within
the period of my life,
I look forward with confidence
to equal advances
by the present generation...

To Benjamin Waterhouse
March 3, 1818

and I have observed this march
of civilisation advancing
from the sea coast, passing over us
like a cloud of light, increasing our
knolege and improving our condition…
and where this progress will stop
no one can say.

To William Ludlow
September 6, 1824

THE WORDS OF
THOMAS JEFFERSON

On Reason

Reason and persuasion
are the only practicable instruments.
To make way for these,
free enquiry must be indulged...

Notes on the State of Virginia
1782

Reason and free enquiry are
the only effectual agents against error.

Notes on the State of Virginia
1782

your own reason is the only oracle
given you by heaven,
and you are answerable
not for the rightness
but uprightness of the decision.

To Peter Carr
August 10, 1787

the example we have given
   to the world is single,
     that of changing
  the form of our government
under the authority of reason only,
    without bloodshed.

To Ralph Izard
July 17, 1788

in every country where
man is free to think & to speak,
differences of opinion will arise
from difference of perception,
& the imperfection of reason.
but these differences, when permitted,
as in this happy country,
to purify themselves
by free discussion…

To Columbia, South Carolina, Citizens
March 23, 1801

every man's own reason
must be his oracle.

To Benjamin Rush
March 6, 1813

this institution [University of Virginia]
will be based on the
illimitable freedom of the human mind.
for here we are not afraid
to follow truth wherever it may lead,
nor to tolerate any error
so long as reason
is left free to combat it.

To William Roscoe
December 27, 1820

…man, once surrendering his reason,
   has no remaining guard against
      absurdities the most monstrous,
and like a ship without rudder
   is the sport of every wind.

To James Smith
December 8, 1822

...in a republican nation
whose citizens are to be led
by reason and persuasion
and not by force,
the art of reasoning becomes
of first importance.

To David Harding
April 20, 1824

THE WORDS OF
THOMAS JEFFERSON

On Religion

…our civil rights have no dependance
on our religious opinions,
any more than on our opinions
in physicks or geometry…

An Act for Establishing
Religious Freedom
1786

…no man shall be compelled
to frequent or support any religious
Worship place or Ministry whatsoever,
nor shall be enforced, restrained,
molested, or burthened in his body
or goods, nor shall otherwise suffer
on account of his religious opinions
or belief…

An Act for Establishing
Religious Freedom
1786

…all men shall be free to profess,
and by argument to maintain
their opinions in matters of religion,
and that the same shall
in no wise diminish, enlarge, or affect
their civil capacities.

**An Act for Establishing
Religious Freedom**
1786

Believing with you that
religion is a matter which lies
solely between Man & his God,
that he owes account
to none other for his faith
or his worship,
that the legitimate powers
of government reach actions only,
& not opinions...

**To the Baptist Association
of Danbury, Connecticut**
January 1, 1802

...I contemplate with
sovereign reverence that act
of the whole American people
which declared that their legislature
should 'make no law respecting
an establishment of religion,
or prohibiting the free exercise thereof,'
thus building a wall of separation
between Church & State.

**To the Baptist Association
of Danbury, Connecticut**
January 1, 1802

I have considered it [religion]
as a matter between every man
and his maker, in which no other,
& far less the public, had a right
to intermeddle.

To Richard Rush
May 31, 1813

…I am a real Christian, that is to say,
a disciple of the doctrines of Jesus…

To Charles Thomson
January 9, 1816

for it is in our lives,
and not from our words,
that our religion must be read.

To Margaret Bayard Smith
August 6, 1816

THE WORDS OF
THOMAS JEFFERSON

On Rights

a bill of rights
is what the people are entitled to
against every government on earth,
general or particular,
and what no just government
should refuse, or rest on inference.

To James Madison
December 20, 1787

I set out on this ground,
which I suppose to be self evident,
'that the earth belongs
in usufruct to the living:'
that the dead have neither
powers nor rights over it.
the portion occupied
by any individual ceases to be his
when himself ceases to be,
& reverts to the society.

To James Madison
September 6, 1789

What is true of every member
of the society individually,
is true of them all collectively,
since the rights of the whole
can be no more than the sum
of the rights of the individuals.

To James Madison
September 6, 1789

for I have sworn
upon the altar of god
    eternal hostility against
every form of tyranny
    over the mind of man.

To Benjamin Rush
September 23, 1800

the principles on which we engaged,
of which the charter
of our independence is the record,
were sanctioned by
the laws of our being, and we but
Obeyed them in pursuing undeviatingly
the course they called for.

To the Republicans of Georgetown
March 8, 1809

I hope & firmly believe
    that the whole world will,
sooner or later, feel benefit
    from the issue of our assertion
      of the rights of man.

To Benjamin Galloway
February 2, 1812

No man has a natural right
to commit aggression
            on the equal rights of another;
and this is all from which
            the laws ought to restrain him...

To Francis Walker Gilmer
June 7, 1816

nothing then is unchangeable
but the inherent and unalienable
rights of man.

To John Cartwright
June 5, 1824

all eyes are opened,
or opening to the rights of man.

To Roger C. Weightman
June 24, 1826

THE WORDS OF
THOMAS JEFFERSON

On Science

…the more ignorant we become
the less value we set on science,
& the less inclination
we shall have to seek it.

To John Adams
May 27, 1795

and I am for encouraging
the progress of science
in all it's branches…

To Elbridge Gerry
January 26, 1799

…every son of science feels
      a strong & disinterested desire
of promoting it in every part
      of the earth…

To Marc Auguste Pictet
February 3, 1803

no body can desire
more ardently than myself
to concur in whatever
may promote useful science,
        and I view no science
with more partiality
        than Natural history.

To Jean de la Coste
May 24, 1807

nature intended me
for the tranquill pursuits of science,
by rendering them my supreme delight.
but the enormities of the times
in which I have lived,
have forced me to take a part
in resisting them, and to commit myself
on the boisterous ocean
of political passions.

To Pierre Samuel Du Pont de Nemours
March 2, 1809

...I endeavor to keep their attention
fixed on the main objects of all science,
the freedom & happiness of man.

To Tadeusz Kosciuszko
February 26, 1810

But even in Europe
a change has sensibly taken place
in the mind of Man.
science had liberated the ideas
of those who read and reflect,
and the American example had kindled
feelings of right in the people.
an insurrection has consequently begun,
of science, talents & courage
against rank and birth,
which have fallen into contempt.

To John Adams
October 28, 1813

an insurrection has consequently begun,
of science, talents & courage
against rank and birth,
which have fallen into contempt...
science is progressive, and
talents and enterprize on the alert.

To John Adams
October 28, 1813

THE WORDS OF
THOMAS JEFFERSON

On Slavery

The whole commerce
　　between master and slave
　is a perpetual exercise
　　　of the most boisterous passions,
the most unremitting despotism
　　　on the one part,
　　　and degrading submissions
　　　on the other.

Notes on the State of Virginia
February 6, 1818

…what an incomprehensible
machine is man! who can endure toil,
famine, stripes, imprisonment
[or] death itself in vindication
of his own liberty, and the next moment…
inflict on his fellow men a bondage,
one hour of which is fraught
with more misery than ages of that
which he rose in rebellion to oppose.

To Jean Nicolas Démeunier
June 26, 1786

I congratulate you, my dear friend,
on the law of your state
for suspending the importation of slaves...
this abomination must have an end,
and there is a superior bench
reserved in heaven
for those who hasten it.

To Edward Rutledge
July 14, 1787

you know that nobody wishes
    more ardently to see an abolition
not only of the trade but
    of the condition of slavery:
and certainly nobody will be
    more willing to encounter
every sacrifice for that object.

To Brissot de Warville
February 11, 1788

...as far as I can judge
    from the experiments
which have been made,
    to give liberty to, or rather,
to abandon persons whose habits
    have been formed in slavery
is like abandoning children.

To Edward Bancroft
January 26, 1789

my opinion has ever been that,
until more can be done for them [slaves],
we should endeavor, with those
whom fortune has thrown on our hands,
to feed & clothe them well,
protect them from ill usage,
require such reasonable labor
only as is performed voluntarily
by freemen, and be led by
no repugnancies to abdicate them,
and our duties to them.

To Edward Coles
August 25, 1814

the love of justice & the love of country
plead equally the cause
of these [enslaved] people,
and it is a mortal reproach to us
that they should have pleaded it
so long in vain, and should have
produced not a single effort...
to relieve them & ourselves
from our present condition
of moral and political reprobation.

To Edward Coles
August 25, 1814

…there is nothing
I would not sacrifice
to a practicable plan of abolishing
every vestige of this moral
and political depravity [slavery].

To Thomas Cooper
September 10, 1814

but this momentous question
[expansion of slavery],
like a fire bell in the night,
awakened and filled me
with terror.

To John Holmes
April 22, 1820

I can say with conscious truth
that there is not a man on earth
who would sacrifice more than I would,
to relieve us from this heavy reproach
[slavery], in any practicable way.

To John Holmes
April 22, 1820

if…a general emancipation
and expatriation could be effected:
and, gradually, and with due sacrifices,
I think it might be. but, as it is,
we have the wolf by the ear,
and we can neither hold him,
nor safely let him go.
justice is in one scale, and
self-preservation in the other.

To John Holmes
April 22, 1820

I considered it
[expansion of slavery] at once
as the knell of the Union.
it is hushed indeed for the moment.
but this is a reprieve only,
not a final sentence.

To John Holmes
April 22, 1820

nothing is more certainly written
in the book of fate than that
these [enslaved] people are to be free.
nor is it less certain that
the two races, equally free,
cannot live in the same government.

Thomas Jefferson
Autobiography
January 6 – July 21, 1821

the abolition of the evil [slavery]
is not impossible:
it ought never therefore to be despaired of.
every plan should be adopted,
every experiment tried,
which may do something
towards the ultimate object.

To Frances Wright
August 7, 1825

THE WORDS OF OTHERS

On Thomas Jefferson

The Governor [Jefferson]
is a most ingenuous
Naturalist and Philosopher,
a truly scientific and learned Man,
and every way excellent.

Ezra Stiles
Literary Diary of Ezra Stiles
1784

You can Scarcely have heard
a Character too high of my Friend
and Colleauge Mr. Jefferson,
either in point of Talent or Virtues.
…I have found him uniformly
the same wise and prudent Man
and Steady Patriot. I only fear that
his unquenchable Thirst for knowledge
may injure his Health.

Henry Knox to John Adams
December 15, 1784

He is Every thing that is Good,
    Up Right, Enlightened, and Clever,
      and is Respected and Beloved
By Every one that knows him.

Lafayette to James McHenry
December 3, 1785

I have found Mr. Jefferson
   a man of infinite information
   and sound Judgment,
becoming gravity, and engaging affability
   mark his deportment.
      His general abilites are such
as would do honor to any age or Country.

Diary of Nathaniel Cutting
September 28 – October 12, 1789

Let me then describe...an American,
who without ever having
quitted his own country,
is Musician, Draftsman, Surveyor,
Astronomer, Natural Philosopher,
Jurist, and Statesman...

Marquis de Chastellux
Travels in North America
April 13, 1792

...no object has escaped Mr. Jefferson;
and it seems as though,
ever since his youth,
he had placed his mind, like his house,
on a lofty height, whence he might
contemplate the whole universe.

Marquis de Chastellux
Travels in North America
April 14 – 16, 1792

Mr. Jefferson...distinguished
as the quiet modest, retiring
philosopher—as the plain simple
unambitious republican.
He shall not now for the first time be
regarded as the intriguing incendiary—
the aspiring turbulent competitor.

Alexander Hamilton
Gazette of the United States
September 29, 1792

Jefferson went off Yesterday,
    and a good riddance of bad ware....
        He has Talents I know,
            and Integrity I believe:
        but his mind is now poisoned
    with Passion, Prejudice and Faction.

John Adams to Abigail Adams
January 6, 1794

[Jefferson] tho wrong in politicks,
      tho formerly an advocate
            for Tom pains Rights of Man,
      and tho frequently mistaken
in Men & measures, I do not
            think him an insincere or
a corruptable Man. my Friendship
      for him has ever been unshaken.

Abigail Adams to John Adams
January 15, 1797

Under the pretence of great indifference
and silence about public measures,
I do now know him [Jefferson]
to be one of the most artful,
intriguing, industrious and double-faced
politicians in all America.

John Nicolas to George Washington
February 22, 1798

Mr Jefferson had the Reputation of a masterly Pen.

John Adams
Autobiography
1804 – 06

The current of his thoughts
is gentle and uniform,
unbroken by the torrent of eloquence,
and unruffled by the fervor
of vivid internal flame.

Joseph Story to Samuel P. P. Fay
March 30, 1807

The Declaration of Independence
I always considered as a theatrical show.
Jefferson ran away
with all the stage effect of that
…and all the glory.

John Adams to Benjamin Rush
June 21, 1811

I consider you and him
as the North and South Poles
of the American Revolution.
Some talked, some wrote, and some
fought to promote and establish it,
but you and Mr. Jefferson
thought for us all.

Benjamin Rush to John Adams
February 17, 1812

Our grandfather seemed
to read our hearts, to see
　　　　our invisible wishes,
to be our good genius,
　　　to wave the fairy wand,
to brighten our young lives
　　　by his goodness and gifts.

Ellen Randolph Coolidge
The Life of Thomas Jefferson
1858

Books were at all times
his chosen companions...he derived
more pleasure from his acquainteance
with Greek and Latin than
from any other resource of literature...

Ellen Randolph Coolidge
quoted in *Literary Diary of Ezra Stiles*
1858

All honor to Jefferson—to the man who,
in the concrete pressure of a struggle
for national independence
by a single people, had the coolness,
forecast, and capacity to introduce
into a merely revolutionary document,
an abstract truth, applicable
to all men and all times...

Abraham Lincoln to
H. L. Pierce and others
April 6, 1859

The fathers of this republic waged
a seven years war for political liberty.
Thomas Jefferson taught me that
my bondage was, in its essence,
worse than ages of that which your fathers
rose in rebellion to oppose.

Frederick Douglass
November 17, 1864

God let loose a thinker
        when Jefferson was born.
...Jefferson's greatness rests
more upon his love of human kind
        than upon his intellect—
            great as was his intellect...
    he was great because his heart was
big enough to embrace the world.

William Jennings Bryan
Master Thoughts of Thomas Jefferson
1907

I think this is the most
extraordinary collection of talent,
of human knowledge,
that has ever been gathered
together at the White House,
with the possible exception of when
Thomas Jefferson dined alone.

John F. Kennedy
Remarks at dinner honoring
Nobel Prize winners
April 29, 1962

ACKNOWLEDGMENTS

THE THOMAS JEFFERSON FOUNDATION, exhibition designers Staples & Charles, and the Small Design Firm conceived the idea for *The Words of Thomas Jefferson* exhibition. What you see on these pages and in the exhibition is the collective effort of curators, historians, editors, designers, and engineers. The first task was to select about two hundred quotations, some well known and others less familiar, from Jefferson's extensive writings. Working with Susan R. Stein, Richard Gilder Senior Curator and Vice President for Museum Programs, Thomas Jefferson Foundation staff contributed their favorites. To be thanked especially are Elizabeth V. Chew, curator of collections; Peter Hatch, director of gardens and grounds; J. Jefferson Looney, editor of the *Papers of Thomas Jefferson: Retirement Series;* and Lucia Stanton, Shannon Senior Historian. Sara Devine, assistant curator of special exhibitions proved invaluable, helping to select quotations and shepherd them through production. Christa Dierskheide, historian and project consultant, also was indispensable. Once selected, the staff of the Retirement Series edited the quotations to make sure that they were transcribed as Jefferson had written them. We are grateful to J. Jefferson Looney and Paula Viterbo, editorial research assistant, whose hard work exceeded what was ever imagined.

Staples & Charles worked with the Small Design Firm, which developed the unique presentation and its software. Staples & Charles designed the bluestone floor with a concentric circular pattern containing the subjects of the exhibition.

Barbara Fahs Charles and Bob Staples, understanding the value of historically appropriate typography, engaged typographer Julian Waters to design a new typeface, ThJefferson, used here for the first time. In addition to David Small, the principal of Small Design Firm, the presentation drew on the talents of Eric Gunther and Justin Manor at Small Design Firm. Jim Gibson, the principal of Gibson Design Associates, designed this book, whose pages echo the projections of the exhibition, and Sarah Allaback coordinated its publication.

We thank the board of trustees of the Thomas Jefferson Foundation and Daniel P. Jordan, president emeritus, for their enthusiastic endorsement of an innovative idea. We honor Donald A. King, Jr. and Janemarie Dionne King, generous friends, who share our excitement for *The Words of Thomas Jefferson*.

LESLIE GREENE BOWMAN
President
Thomas Jefferson Foundation